THE
NEW YORKER
BOOK OF KIDS* CARTOONS

*and the people who live with them

BLOOMBERG PRESS

PRINCETON

THE
NEW YORKER
BOOK OF KIDS* CARTOONS

*and the people who live with them

EDITED BY ROBERT MANKOFF

INTRODUCTION BY ROZ CHAST

MS
741.5
NEW

5/01

PUBLISHED BY BLOOMBERG PRESS

Copyright © 2001 by The New Yorker Magazine, Inc.

All art is protected by registrations and renewals duly filed with the Register of Copyrights, Library of Congress, by The New Yorker Magazine, Inc.

The magazine's name and logo are protected by registrations duly filed with the Patent and Trademark Office, and in trademark registries abroad.

All rights reserved. Protected under the Berne Convention. Printed in the United States of America. No part of this book may be reproduced, stored in a retrieval system, or transmitted, in any form or by any means, electronic, mechanical, photocopying, recording, or otherwise, without the prior written permission of CARTOONBANK.COM except in the case of brief quotations embodied in critical articles and reviews. For information, please write: Permissions Department, Bloomberg Press, 100 Business Park Drive, P.O. Box 888, Princeton, NJ 08542-0888 U.S.A.

To purchase framed prints of cartoons or to license cartoons for use in periodicals, Web sites, or other media, please contact CARTOONBANK.COM, a New Yorker Magazine company, at 145 Palisade Street, Suite 373, Dobbs Ferry, NY 10522, Tel: 800-897-TOON, or (914) 478-5527, Fax: (914) 478-5604, e-mail: toon@cartoonbank.com, Web: www.cartoonbank.com.

Books are available for bulk purchases at special discounts. Special editions or book excerpts can also be created to specifications. For information, please write: Special Markets Department, Bloomberg Press.

BLOOMBERG, THE BLOOMBERG, BLOOMBERG NEWS, BLOOMBERG FINANCIAL MARKETS, and BLOOMBERG PRESS are trademarks and service marks of Bloomberg L.P. All rights reserved.

First edition published 2001
1 3 5 7 9 10 8 6 4 2

Library of Congress Cataloging-in-Publication Data

The New Yorker book of kids cartoons / edited by Robert Mankoff ; introduction by Roz Chast.
    p. cm.
    On t.p. "kids" is followed by an asterisk that refers to "and the people who live with them". Includes index.
    ISBN 1-57660-097-1 (alk. paper)
    1. Children--Caricatures and cartoons. 2. Parent and child--Caricatures and cartoons. 3. American wit and humor, Pictorial. 4. New Yorker (New York, N.Y. : 1925) I. Title: Book of kids cartons, II. Mankoff, Robert. III. New Yorker (New York, N.Y. : 1925)

NC1763.C45 N48 2001
741.5'973--dc21
                                                2001037380

Book design by LAURIE LOHNE / Design It Communications

THE
NEW YORKER
BOOK OF KIDS* CARTOONS

*and the people who live with them

INTRODUCTION

BY ROZ CHAST

Some people like to imagine that the Family is a wellspring of inspiration for an artist. I think of it, as a parent of children and as a child of parents, as The Bottomless Pit. But why quibble? Perhaps, for cartoonists, it's six of one, half a dozen of the other.

When I was a kid, my parents subscribed to *The New Yorker*. I didn't read it back then—too many words, not enough pictures. But I used to love to look at the cartoons. Most of them I sort of got. Some of them I didn't get at all. But the ones I really loved were the ones about kids—kids talking to other kids, kids just by themselves, kids at the beach, kids in school, parents and kids ... all of them. I didn't know what a board meeting was, and the cocktail party genre didn't do a lot for me, but I did know two things: (1) that families definitely had their grimly funny moments and (2) that kids saw the world a lot differently from adults. The kid-related cartoons in *The New Yorker* were one of the few places where I saw adults admitting these truths.

Here you are, grown-up or child or somewhere in between, reading this introduction. But where were you before you dropped into your respective family? Perhaps you were a disembodied spirit, capering around in an Elysian Field. Then, in the midst of your capering, you came upon this big hole in the ground that you had never seen before. Nearby there was a sign: STAND BACK FIFTY FEET. Did you pay attention to the sign? Of course not. That's a sign for dunderheads, and since you're an exceptionally intelligent—and curious—Spirit, it doesn't apply to you. Uh-oh! You shouldn't have leaned over so far! #$%*#%! There you go, tumbling into the hole, falling, falling, falling—until the next thing you know, you are ... born.

Standing near you are these two large people with bad breath. They mean well, but they're soooo annoying. The only thing that changes over the next twenty or so years is that they will get even more annoying, and you will get smarter.

THIS IS YOUR CHILDHOOD

Finally, when you can no longer bear it, you will move out. You will have a few good, family-free years. You will be finding yourself, eating black pasta, watching experimental movies, sleeping on a futon, and so forth. Then, one day, years after you've seen that film in health class, *Your Wondrous, Changing Body*, you'll meet somebody extra special. BAM!! Say goodbye to your black pasta years, because before you know it, you'll be in the middle of your own family, except this one is YOUR fault. It all begins again. You, your mate, your kids, bunched around the dinner table, or collapsed on the sofa in a semicoma staring at the TV—hashing everything out and trying hard not to kill each other in the process.

If you don't want to go off your rocker in a very short period of time, I suggest trying to find as much of your family experience as funny as you can. Sometimes it's very easy because kids actually DO say the darndest things. The other day, a friend of mine told me about the time her six-year-old became entranced by a hugely obese woman standing just a couple of feet away in the supermarket. "Look, Mommy! Look at that really FAT LADY! Have you ever seen anybody so FAT? MOM! LOOK HOW FAT SHE IS!" "Don't call her 'fat,' sweetheart—that might hurt her feelings." Five minutes later: *"THERE SHE IS AGAIN!"* But, see: She didn't call her "fat," so it's OK.

For some reason it's harder when it's you saying the darndest things. Not long ago, my family and I were sitting around the table eating dinner. My son had recently seen a suspenseful movie with a couple of his pals and decided to describe the entire plot. It was a movie that I was hoping to see myself, so I asked him—politely, respectfully—if he would terribly mind not sharing the ending, because part of the fun for me was not knowing what was going to happen next, hence, the thrill of suspense. He was quiet for a couple of seconds, but then it was like that scene in *The Simpsons* where Bart's teacher bends over and there's her big behind, just waving in the air, and Bart has a spitball. My son looked at me and said, "And then, in the end, they all die." Suddenly, I just started screaming at him: "I can't believe you told me when I specifically asked you NOT to! I ask you for one TEENY, TINY THING! I never ask you for ANYTHING! FUCK YOU!" Then I picked up the hot dog from my plate (we were having hot dogs that night—nothing's too good for MY family) and threw it at him as hard as I could.

Now, believe it or not, we are not a cursing, hot-dog-throwing family. And my parents never swore at or threw food at me, much less both at once, so I can't even blame my behavior on them, the way I like to. In any case, it was so astonishing that after the first couple of horrible, silent minutes, we were all laughing like maniacs. The kids still remember it: "Remember when Mom threw the hot dog and said the *F* word? HA HA HA—and it was over a stupid MOVIE! HA HA HA HA HA HA." I'm just grateful that when the dust—or the hot dog—had settled, we could still say, like the fish in Sam Gross's cartoon on page 47: "I guess we'd be considered a family. We're living together, we love each other, and we haven't eaten the children yet."

People are always asking cartoonists, "Where do you get your ideas?" They might answer, "the news," or "something funny someone said," or "Home Depot." Or perhaps they just finished having a dialog like this:

You stand there and think, "Should I drive back to Blockbuster and look for the sneaker? It's far away, and I have other things I'd much rather do. Plus, the sneaker will probably be gone. Should I punish him? How would I punish him for losing a sneaker? Take away the other sneaker? Then he'll walk around in just socks, and the socks will get filthy, and I'll have to throw those away, and he might even step on a rusty nail and—wait a minute, are his tetanus shots up to date? Isn't there some kind of booster shot he's supposed to get?" By the time you've decided how to handle it perfectly, you'll have used up thousands of brain cells and you'll be even farther down that Bottomless Pit than you were before.

Just keep in mind: if you think you are powerless, think how your child feels. Both of my kids are constantly amazed at how many hours out of their lives they have to spend in school. When they question me about it, it's hard to say anything other than the extremely lame "It's the LAW." And unless they go to one of those extra special schools where there are four kids in a class and it's self-expression-a-plenty, not only must they GO to school, but they have to memorize lists of prepositions, learn what a cosine is, take tests on boring books they never wanted to read in the first place, and do reasonably well at these tasks so that you, the parent, do not throw a conniption fit.

When the school day is over, they're still not free. As the kid in Robert Weber's cartoon on page 4 says, "There's a lot of pressure to be good." The second they get home, it's: Why is the mayonnaise still on the counter? Who left this jacket on the floor? Did you brush your teeth? How was that science test? When are you going to send in that application? Is that your fifth soda? How many times have I told you: "NO MORE THAN TWO PEOPLE AT ONCE ON THE TRAMPOLINE"? Did you thank Grandma for the flannel sheets? How are you getting home from Fred's party? Will Fred's parents be there? Are you sure Fred's parents don't keep guns in the house? Absolutely sure? After all that, what choice does a kid have but to get a great big ganja leaf tattooed on his or her back so that when your family goes to Florida to see the grandparents, there'll be a lot of explaining to do? Basically, when you're a kid, you are the baby chick in Lee Lorenz's cartoon on page 11 who finally hatches from his shell, only to have his mother point to the broken pieces and say, "NOW look what you've done."

So let's face it. We're all falling down the same hole: you, me, your kids, my kids, my kids' kids, my spouse, your spouse, my parents, your parents, that fat lady in the supermarket, and countless, countless others. If something makes us laugh along the way, as my mother would say, it can't hurt.

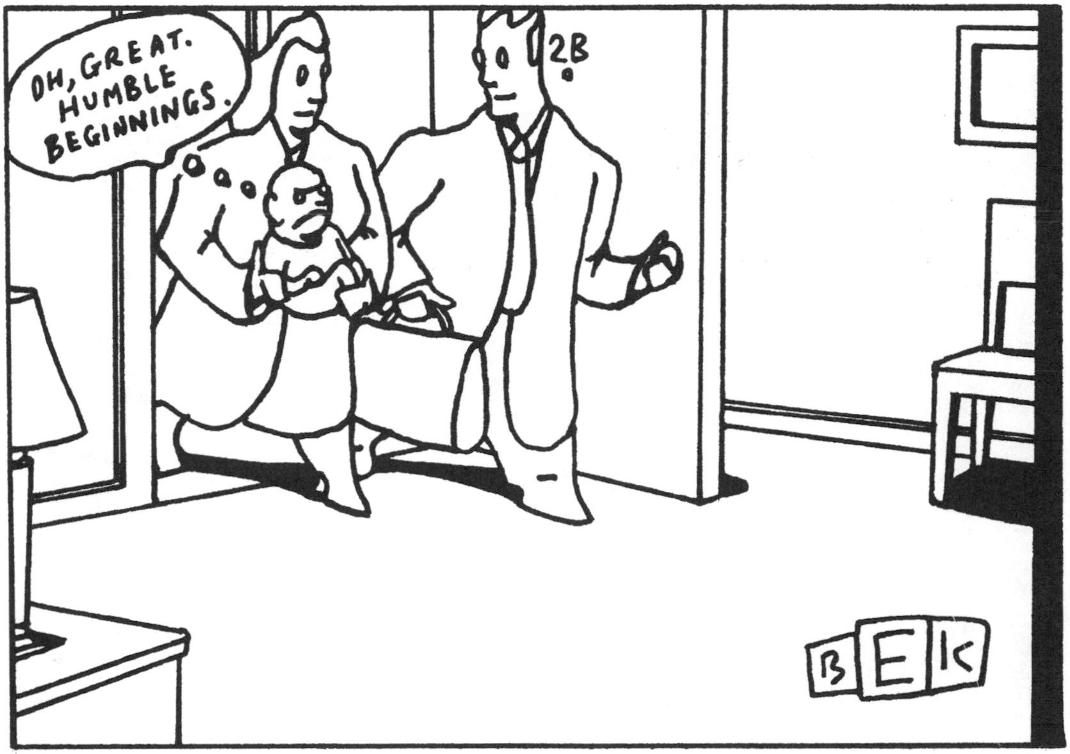
OH, GREAT. HUMBLE BEGINNINGS.
2B
BEK

CAST OF DREAM
THE MONSTER...... YOUR FATHER
KIND WOMAN...... YOUR MOTHER
POLICEMAN .... YOUR ANALYST
FIRST STRANGER.... YOUR BROTHER
SECOND STRANGER .. YOUR SISTER
LITTLE BOY..... YOU
Dana Fradon

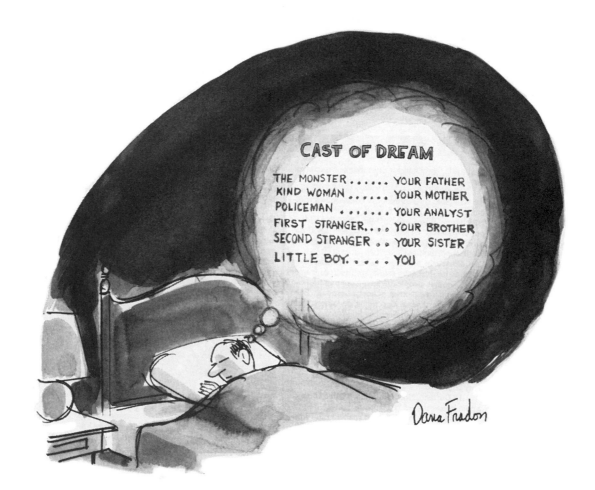

"Is everything all right, Jeffrey? You never call me 'dude' anymore."

"I find there's a lot of pressure to be good."

"*What do I think is an appropriate punishment?
I think an appropriate punishment would
be to make me live with my guilt.*"

"Why can't you be more like little Hester Prynne? She's getting straight As."

"Don't trample on a young girl's hopes and dreams, Roy."

THE BERLITZ GUIDE TO PARENT - TEACHER CONFERENCES

TEACHERESE	ENGLISH
Marches to a different drummer.	Nuts.
Needs to brush up on his people skills.	Homicidal.
Creative.	None too bright.
Very creative.	A moron, actually.
She's a riot!	I can't stand her.
He's doing just fine.	What's your kid's name again?

R. Chast

"Can't I just stay here with you and Mom? I don't like what I've seen of the real world."

"*I think he's finally asleep.*"

"Now look what you've done!"

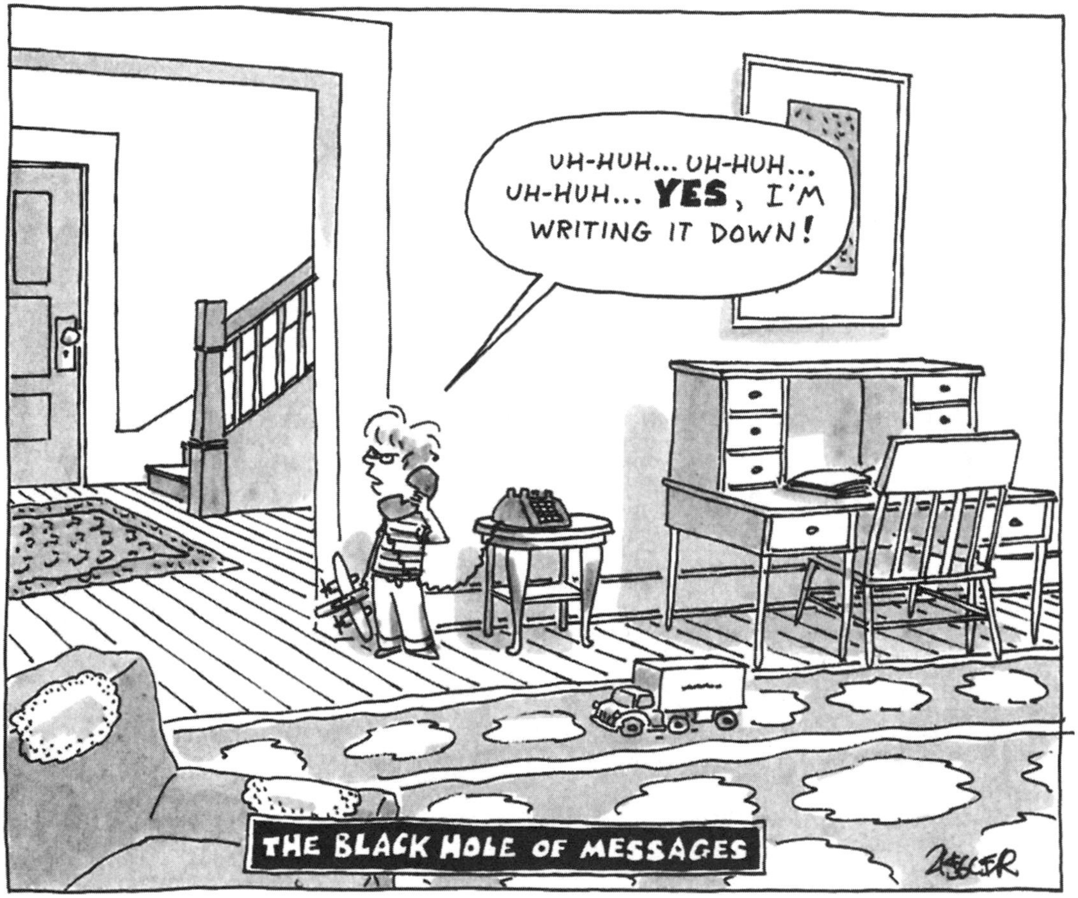
UH-HUH... UH-HUH... UH-HUH... YES, I'M WRITING IT DOWN!
THE BLACK HOLE OF MESSAGES

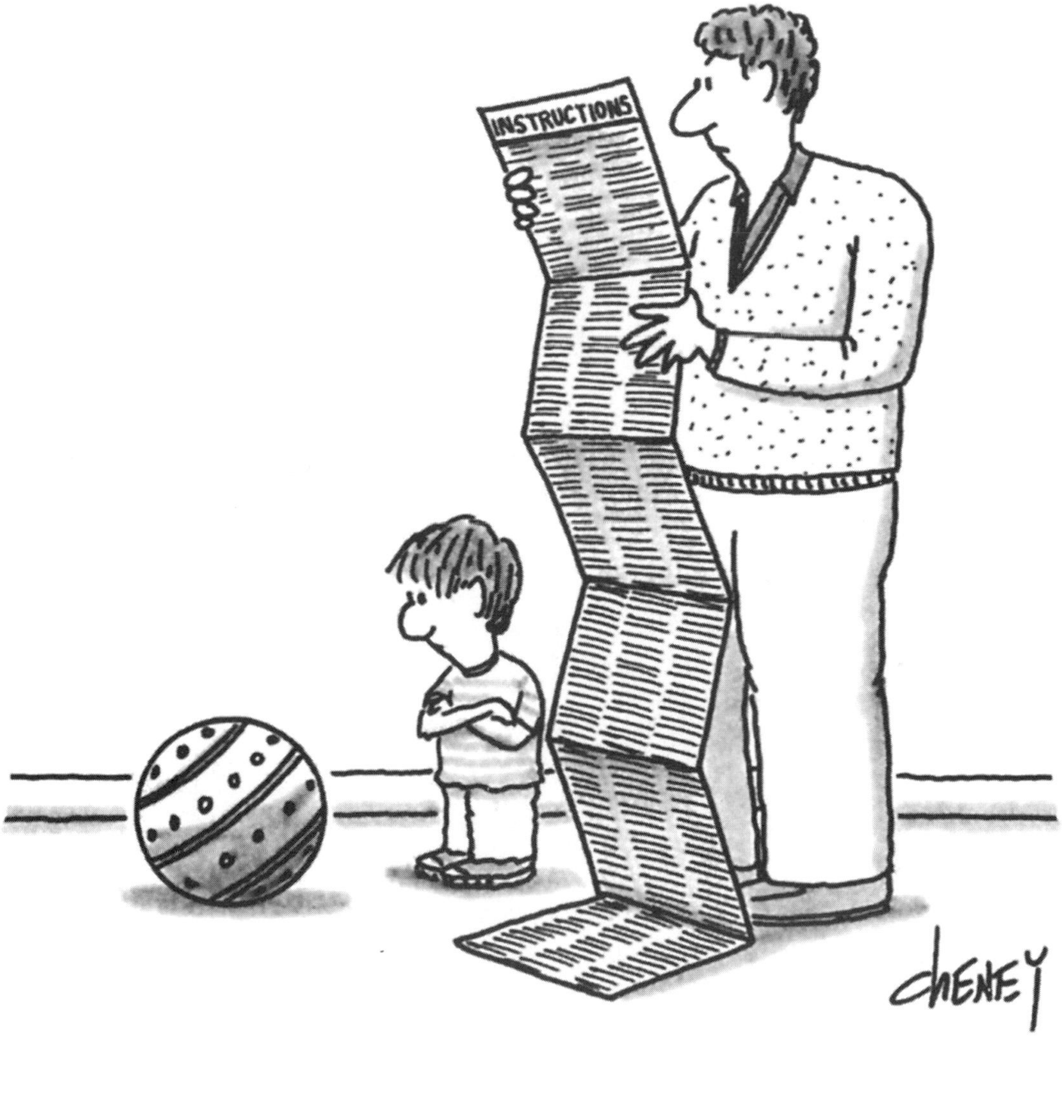
INSTRUCTIONS
cheney

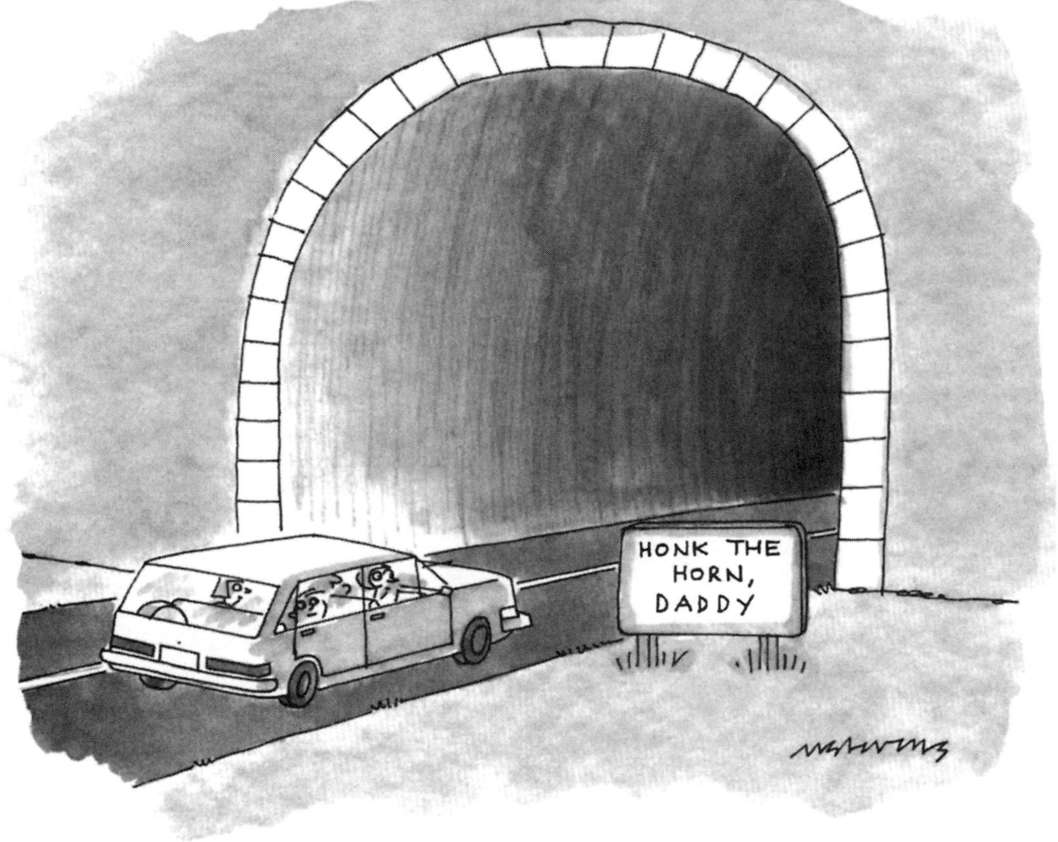
HONK THE
HORN,
DADDY

"Felicia, both your father and I feel you're too young to be mysterious."

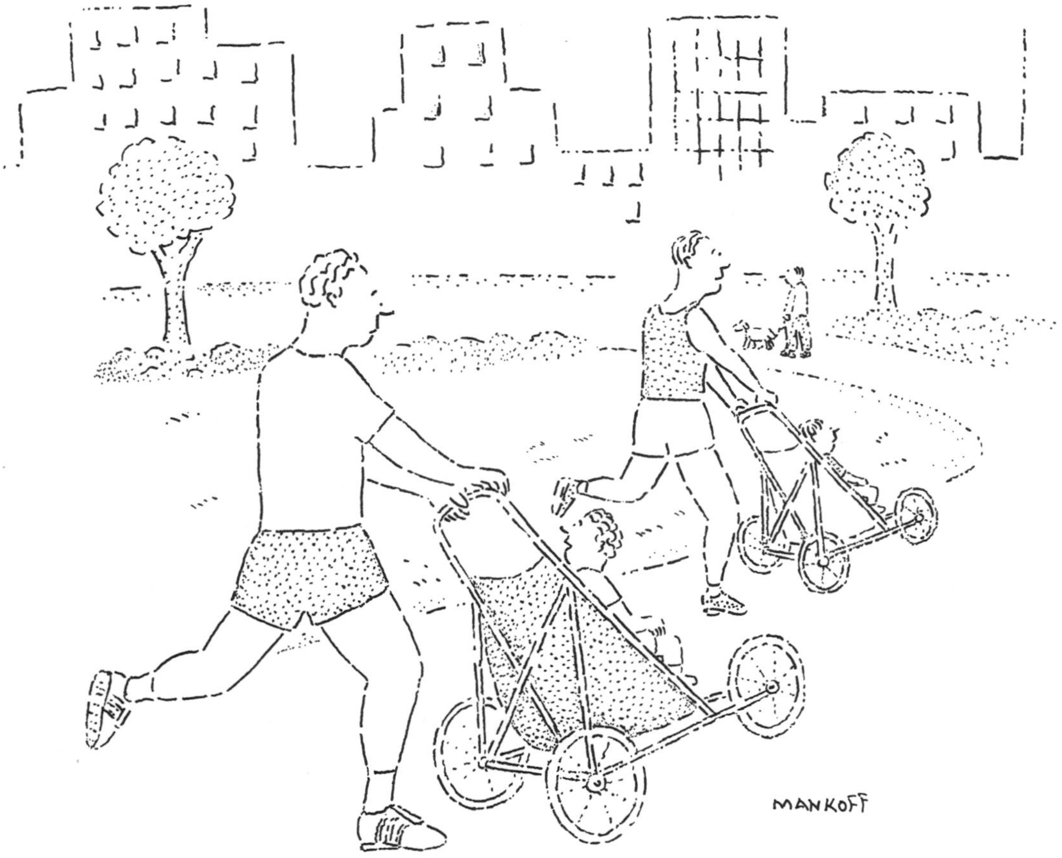
MANKOFF

"Pass 'em, Pop."

"The little dears! They still believe in Santa Claus."

"It's so much easier now that the children are our age."

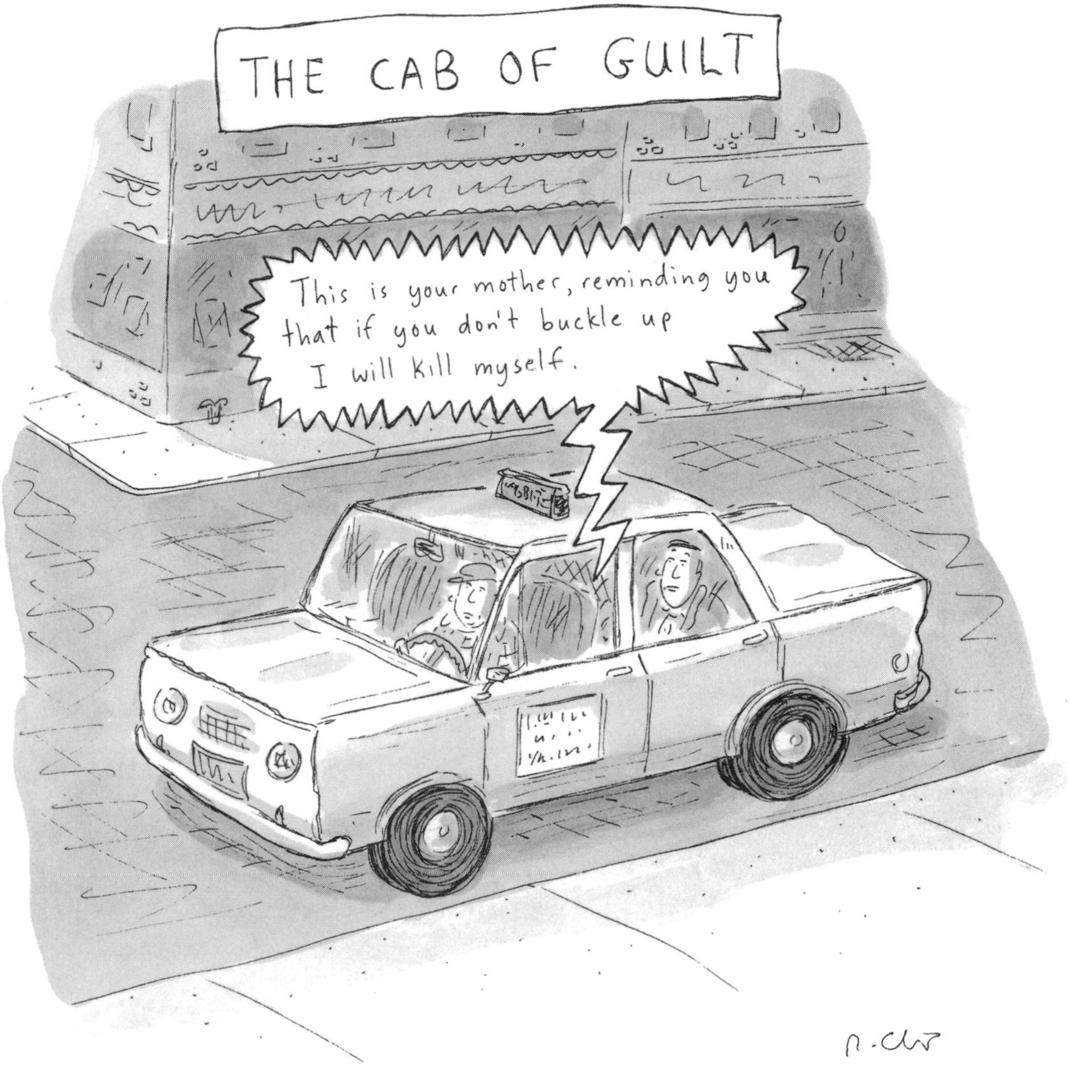
THE CAB OF GUILT
This is your mother, reminding you that if you don't buckle up I will kill myself.

"So, are you still with the same parents?"

"*Stop asking so many questions, or it's right back to Books on Tape for you.*"

"Daddy promises he'll be there the next time you kick butt, honey."

"Stop calling! We'll get there when we get there!"

"If it's not safe to go in the water and it's not safe to go in the sun,
why did you bring me here?"

"I don't usually go to parties, but I'm very fond of Aaron."

"Dad, I need to dip into my college fund."

"So, what's your custody deal?"

"Dad, can you read?"

"O.K., who has to go potty before we disappear into the Federal Witness Protection Program?"

"O.K., you be the doctor, and I'll be the Secretary of Health and Human Services."

"*Mom always liked you and Pinkie and Spike and Custard and Fluffy best.*"

PLAYING THE YOUTH CARD

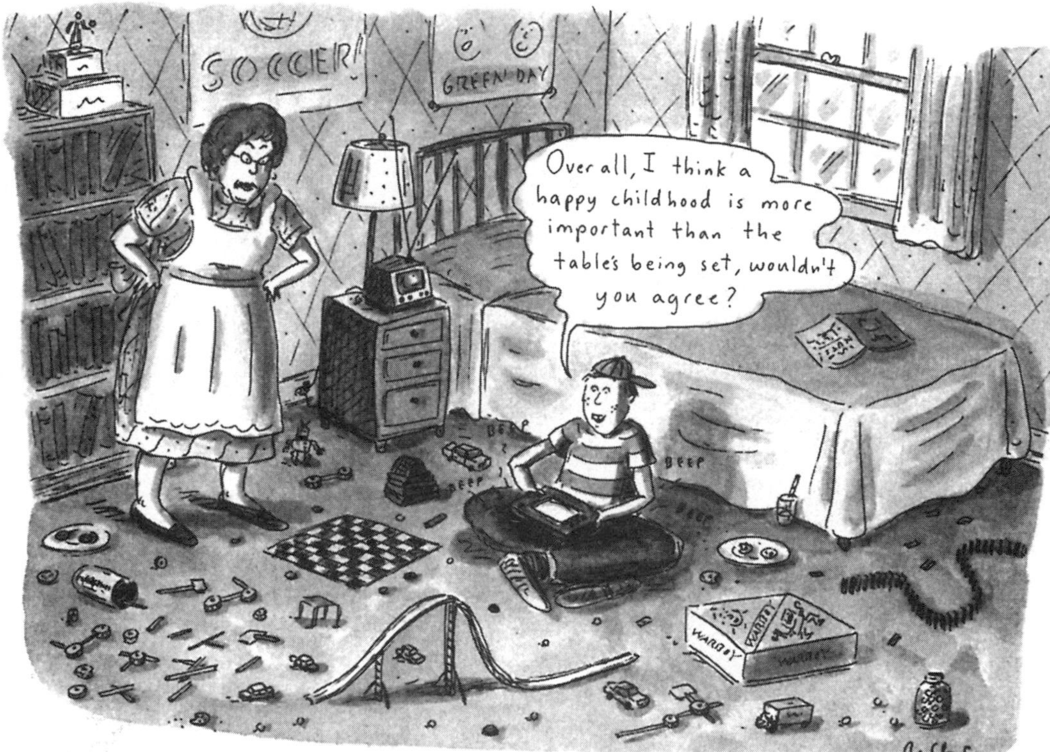
SOCCER
GREEN DAY
Overall, I think a happy childhood is more important than the table's being set, wouldn't you agree?
BEEP

"Never, ever do that again!"

"I've had a long talk with Jonah, and I think he's willing to work with us."

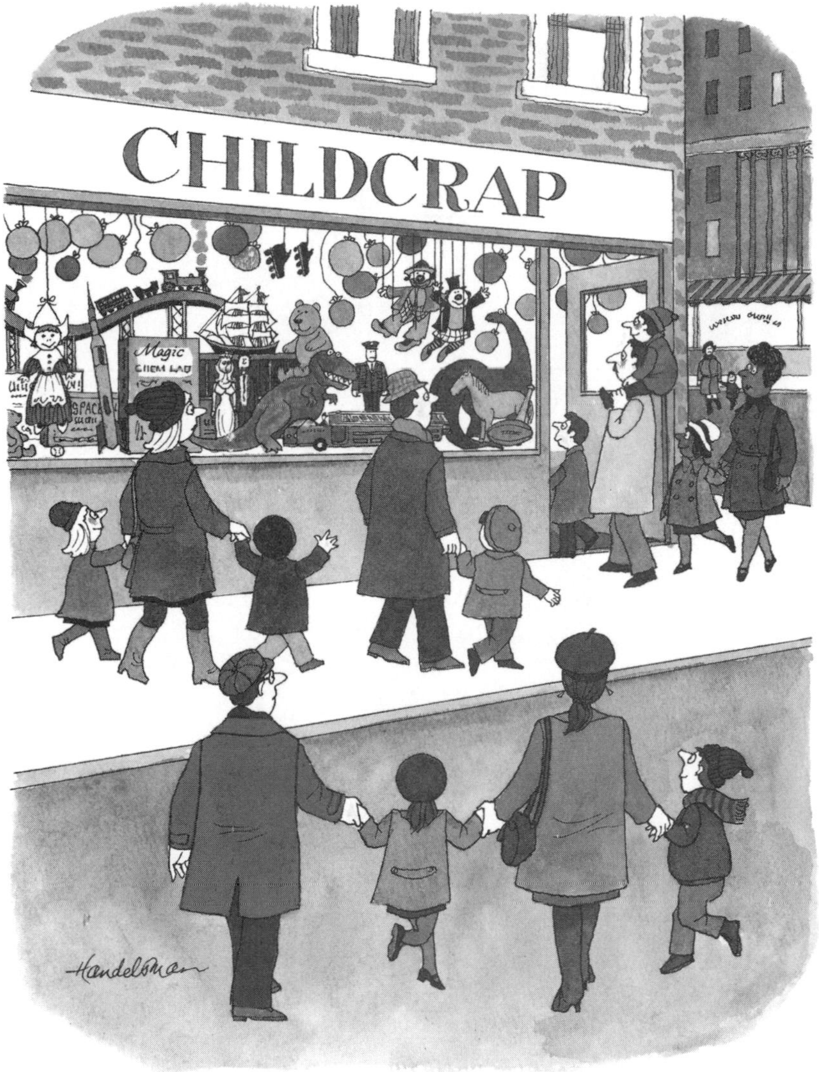
CHILDCRAP
Magic
SPACE
Handelsman

"*You'd better ask your grandparents about that, son—my generation is very uncomfortable talking about abstinence.*"

"I _know_ sex is no longer a taboo subject. I just don't feel like
discussing it all the time, that's all."

"Dad, when did you realize you weren't, you know, exactly studly anymore?"

"Big deal, an A in math. That would be a D in any other country."

"... and please keep me from falling out of bed again tonight."

"That's not white noise. That's the ocean."

"I still don't have all the answers, but I'm beginning to ask the right questions."

"Attention, please. At 8:45 A.M. on Tuesday, July 29, 2025, you are all scheduled to take the New York State Bar Exam."

"You call that hung by the chimney with care?"

"Boy, did $\underline{I}$ have an afternoon! The census man was here."

"*According to this analysis, Gibbons, last year your department spent forty-five thousand dollars on candy alone.*"

"I guess we'd be considered a family. We're living together, we love each other, and we haven't eaten the children yet."

"Dad, you can't expect to pick up the basics of the new math
in a simple dinner-table conversation."

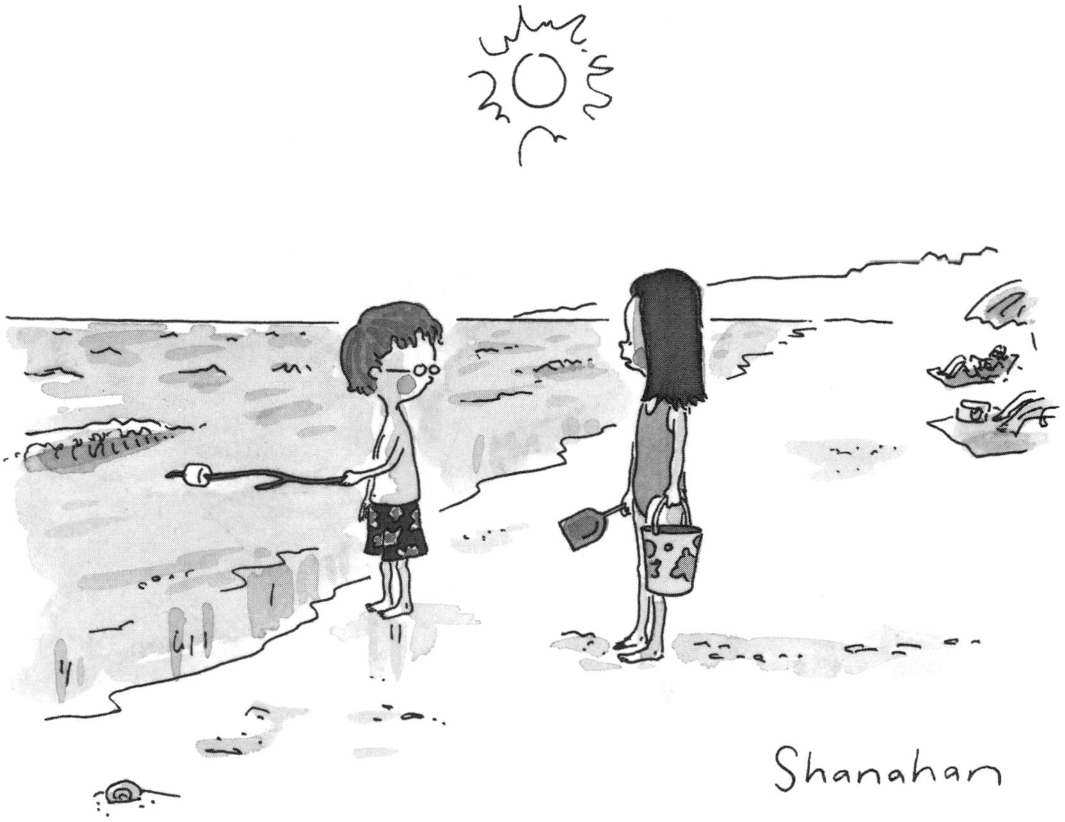
Shanahan

"First beach?"

BAD MOM® CARDS
COLLECT THE ENTIRE SET!
#4: ESTHER J.
Ran out of orange juice one morning and served kids orange soda instead.
#17: GLORIA B.
Promised to take daughter to the mall after school- and then didn't.
#20: JAYNE R.
SPRING VALLEY SCHOOL
Sent child to school with 99.1°F. temperature - and child was sent home.
#23: LUCY L.
And then he...
Told friend "funny" story about kid and had a laugh at kid's expense.
#35: MARTINA F.
EASTER
ST. PATRICK'S
XMAS
Didn't put up the St. Patrick's Day decorations one year.
#39: DAWN K.
When daughter left stuffed bear in Grand Union, waited until next day to retrieve it.
#48: SUZIE M.
Let kid play two hours of Nintendo- just to get him out of her hair.
#61: DEBORAH Z.
Has never even tried to make Play-Doh from scratch.
#89: BECKY O.
While on phone, told child to SHUT THE HELL UP, or she would brain her.
R. Chast

"O.K., here I am in the fourth grade, but is that really what I want to be doing with my life?"

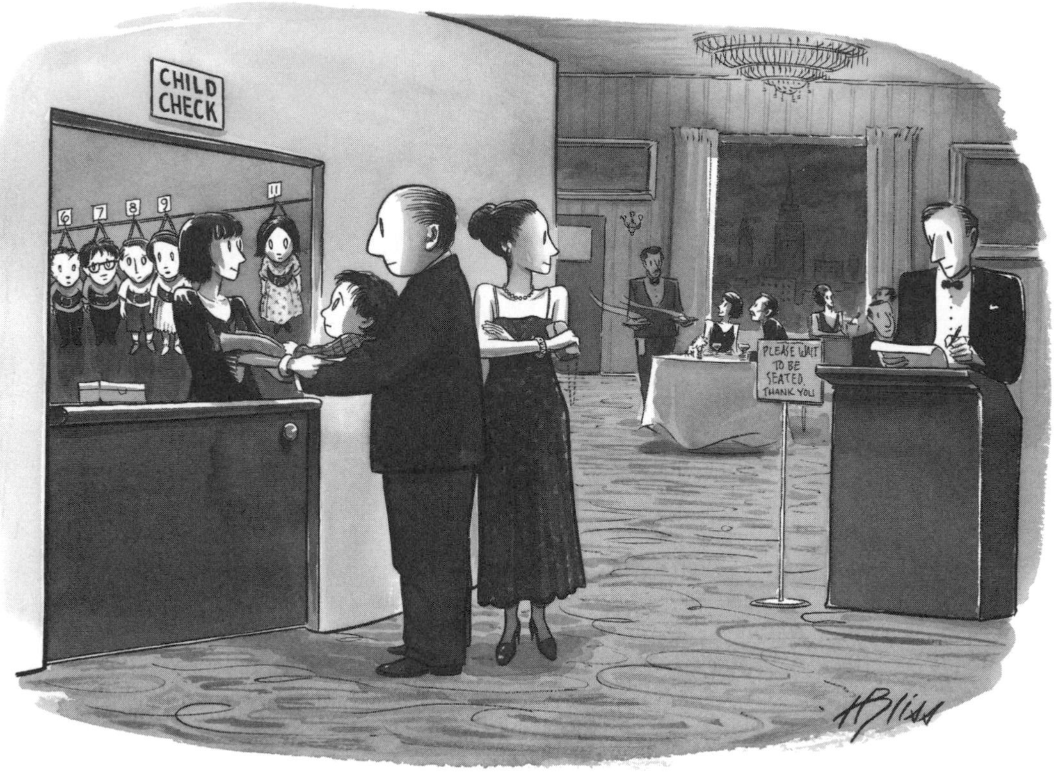
CHILD CHECK
6
7
8
9
11
PLEASE WAIT TO BE SEATED. THANK YOU

"Mike, I have to level with you. I said I liked Disney World, but actually I didn't."

"Don't sweat it. That's Little League—your dad comes, you choke."

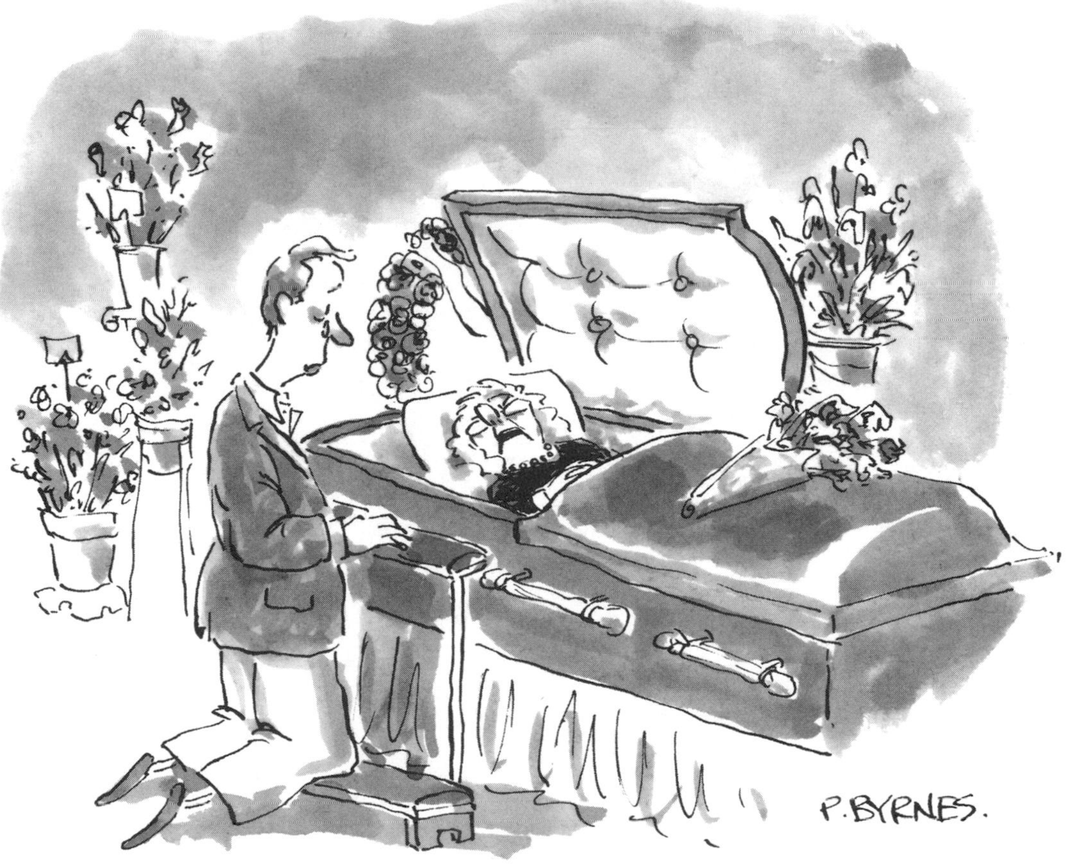
P. BYRNES.

"You couldn't put on a tie?"

"Mom, I am not a billionaire! A billion is like a thousand million. I'm worth a hundred million. A hundred million is just a hundred million."

"If you're not a good boy, Santa will bring you only educational toys."

"*I love you too, Daddy, but it just kills me that you're a man.*"

"*Your daughter is a pain in the ass.*"

THE DREAM REMOTE

WAKE UP
BRUSH YOUR TEETH
TAKE A SHOWER
MAKE YOUR BED
SLOWER
COMB YOUR HAIR
CHANGE THAT AWFUL SHIRT
FASTER
CALL GRANDMA
SET TABLE
TAKE OUT GARBAGE
WRITE THANK-YOU NOTE
TURN THAT MUSIC OFF
CLEAN ROOM
DO HOMEWORK
EAT VEGETABLE
PUT THAT DOWN
PICK THAT UP
LEAVE THAT ALONE
STOP PICKING ON YOUR BROTHER OR SISTER
DEAL WITH THE DOG—HE'S YOUR RESPONSIBILITY
GO TO BED

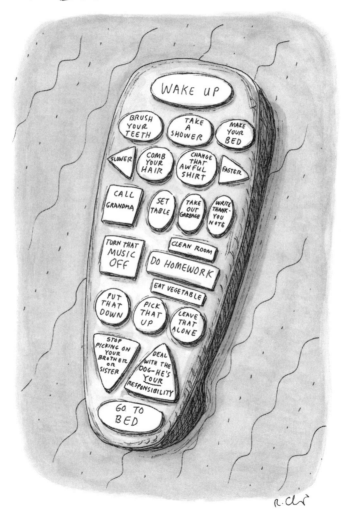

"Son, your mother and I think that you are now old enough to get your own drink of water."

"Hey, look—Mom left us an internal memo."

"Have some respect for my learning style."

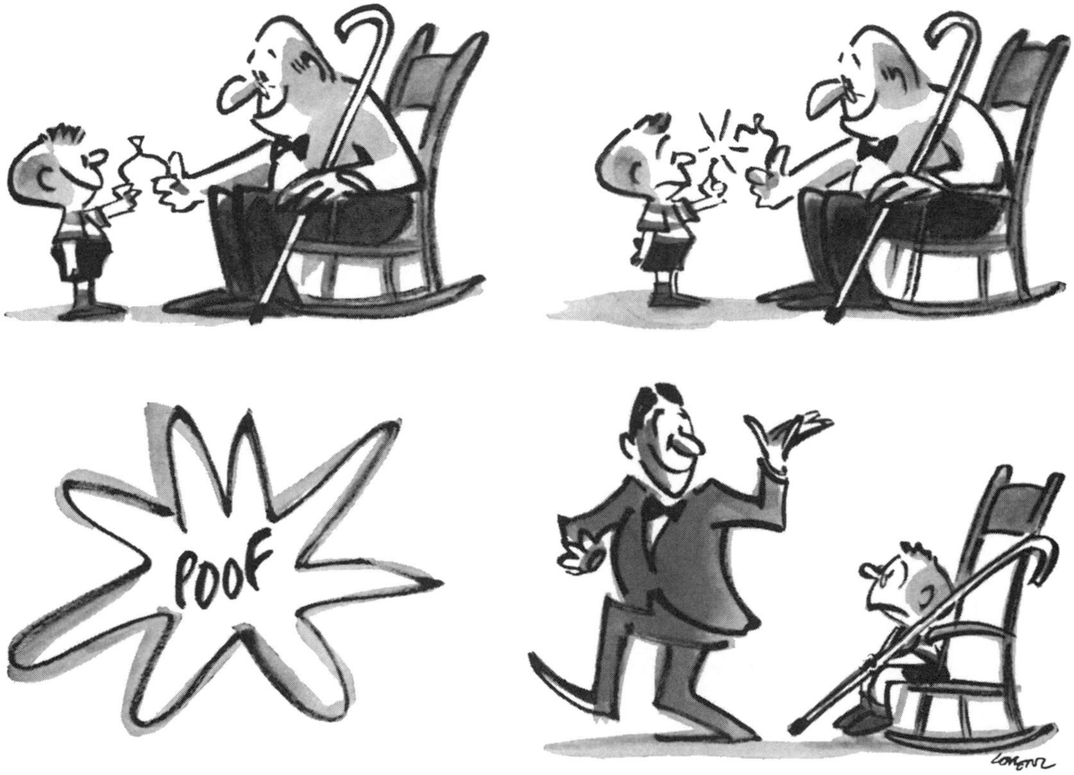
POOF
LORENZ

"He's just doing that to get attention."

"I'd like more child support."

"While we're at supper, Billy, you'd make Daddy and Mommy very happy
if you'd remove your hat, your sunglasses, and your earring."

"Your mother and I are feeling overwhelmed, so you'll have to bring yourselves up."

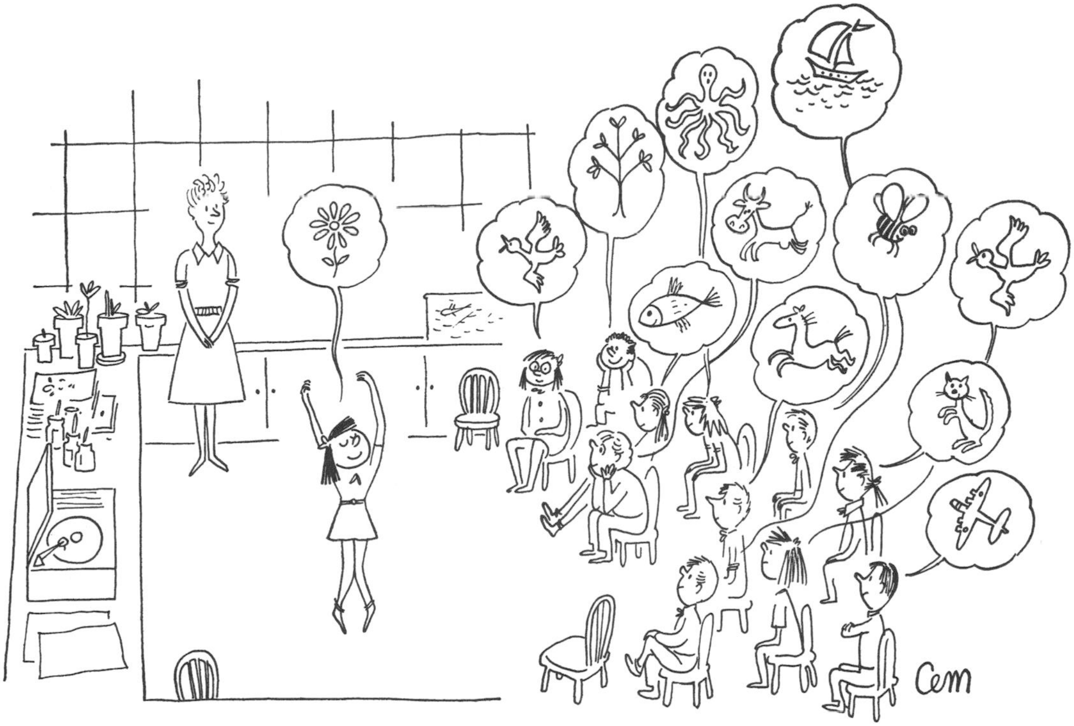
Cem

"_That's_ what's the matter with kids today!"

"Please, Mrs. Enright, if I let you pinch-hit for Tommy,
all the mothers will want to pinch-hit."

"Someday, sweetheart, all of this will belong to your ex–husband and his attorney."

"We're really bonding now, aren't we, Dad?"

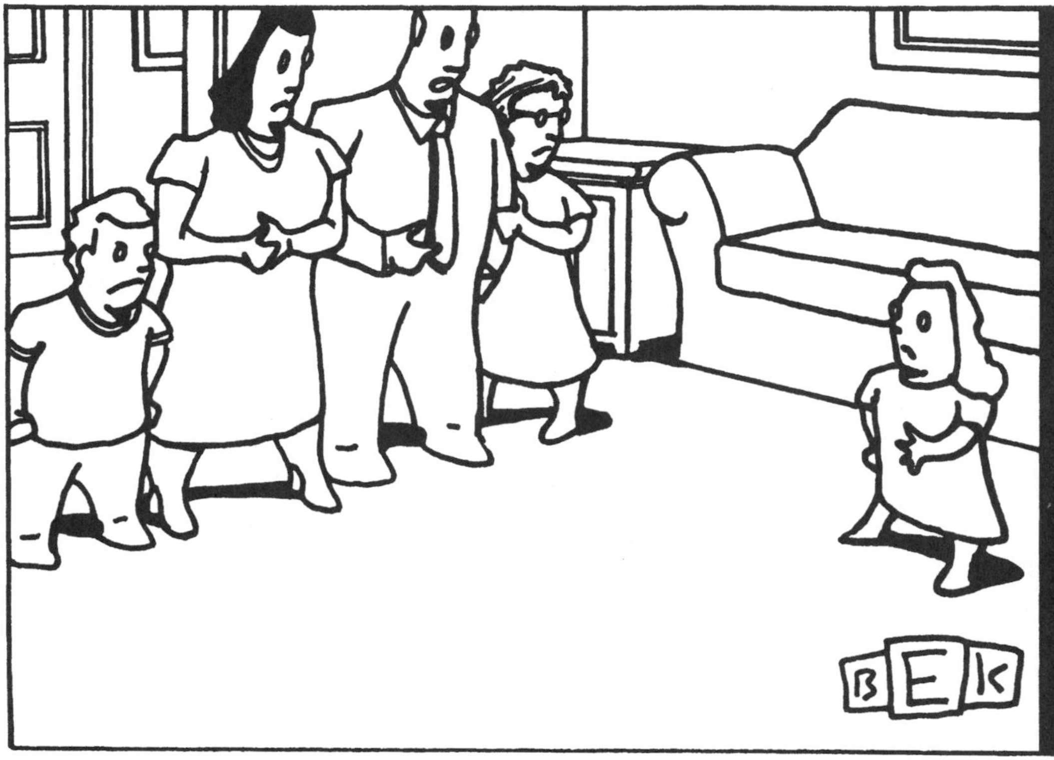
BEK

"Bad news—we're all out of our minds. You're going to have to be the lone healthy person in this family."

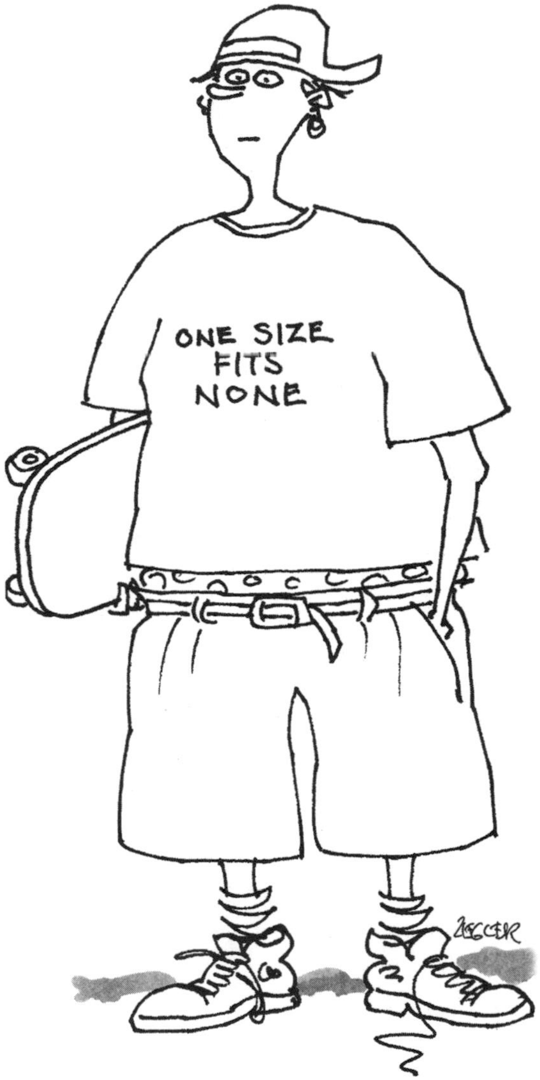
ONE SIZE
FITS
NONE

"It's broccoli, dear."
"I say it's spinach, and I say the hell with it."

"I say it's genetically altered, and I say the hell with it."

"I know more about art than you do, so I'll tell you what to like."

"*Thank you, Adrian. Parenting is a learning process, and your criticisms help.*"

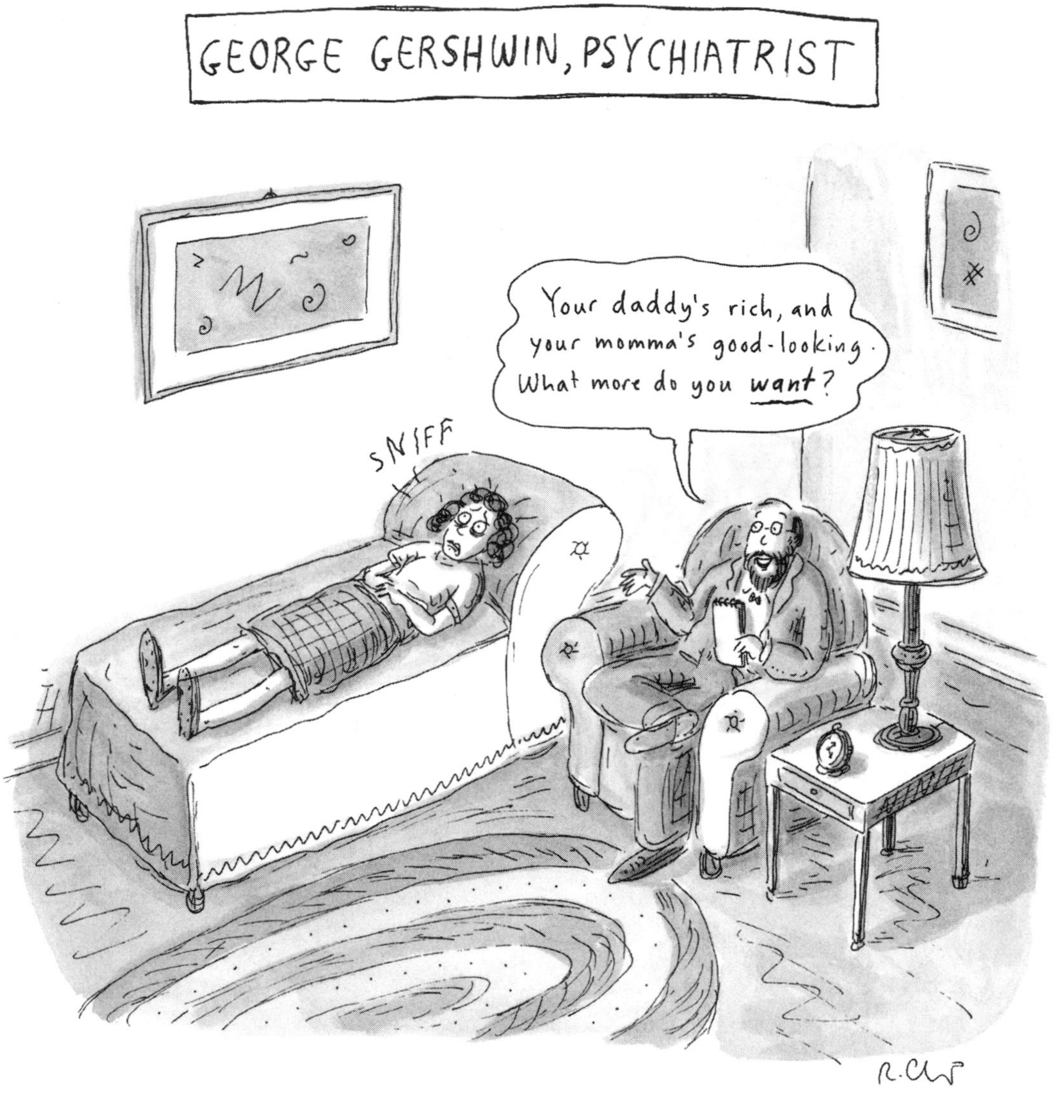
GEORGE GERSHWIN, PSYCHIATRIST
Your daddy's rich, and your momma's good-looking. What more do you want?
SNIFF

"Oh, he's cute, all right, but he's got the temperament of a car alarm."

"Dad, remember how you bungled the Lorton account?"

"And then, as soon as I had carved out my niche,
they went and had another kid."

"It sounds a little too perfect. What's the downside?"

"*I hope you realize that I'm the one who has to write about this stupid vacation next fall.*"

"The minute you walked into the room, I said to myself, 'Now, *he* looks interesting.'"

"All you really need in life is the love of a good cat."

"My mom and dad are still very sharp."

"I hope you kept the box it came in."

"And so, kids, if you don't find this awesome new game under the tree, you've really got to ask yourselves what you're doing there."

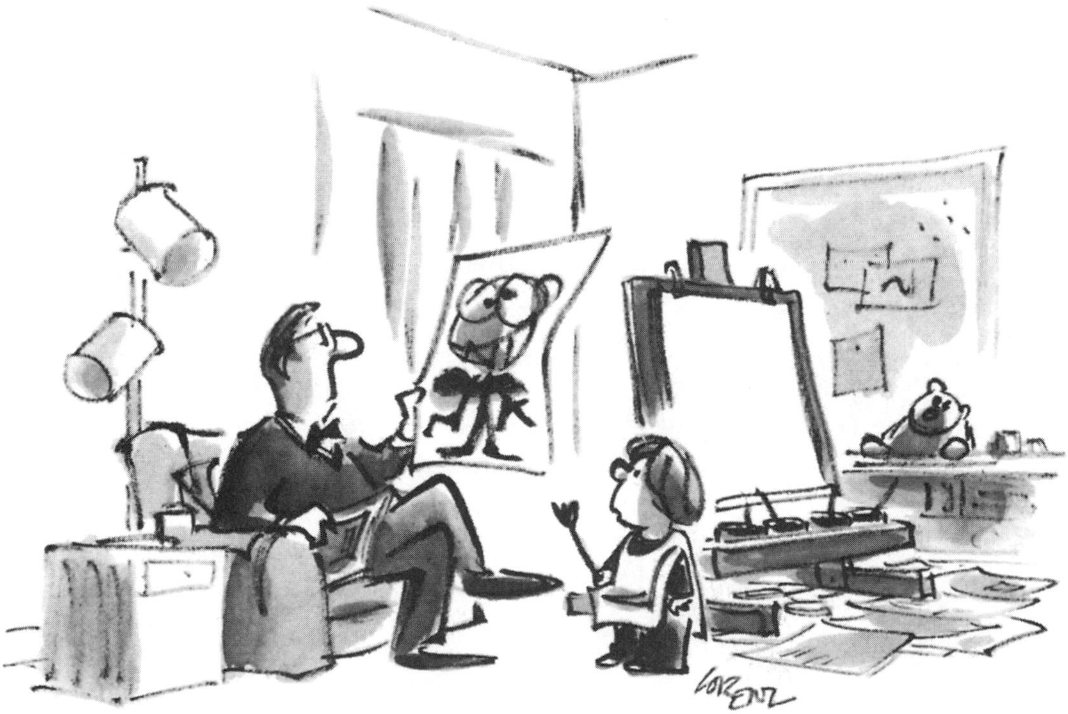
LORENZ

"You moved."

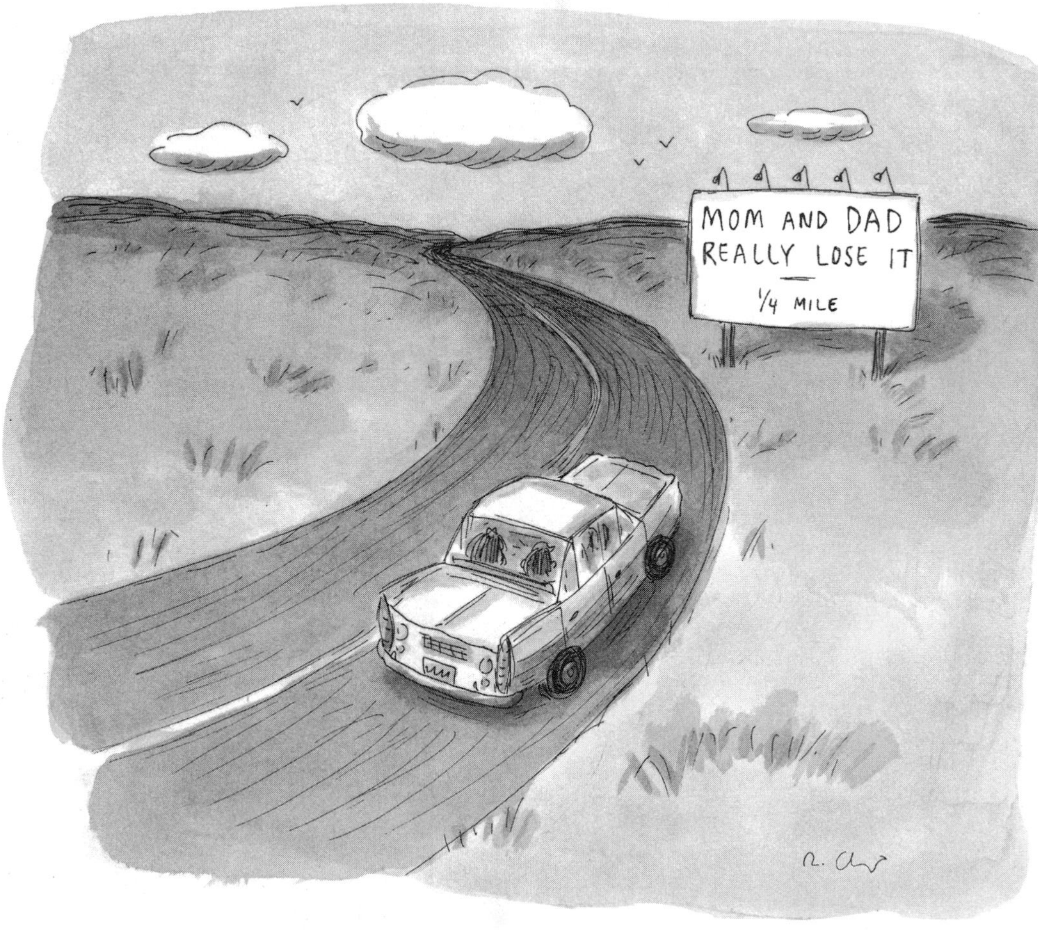
MOM AND DAD
REALLY LOSE IT
1/4 MILE

"*This is gonna hurt like hell.*"

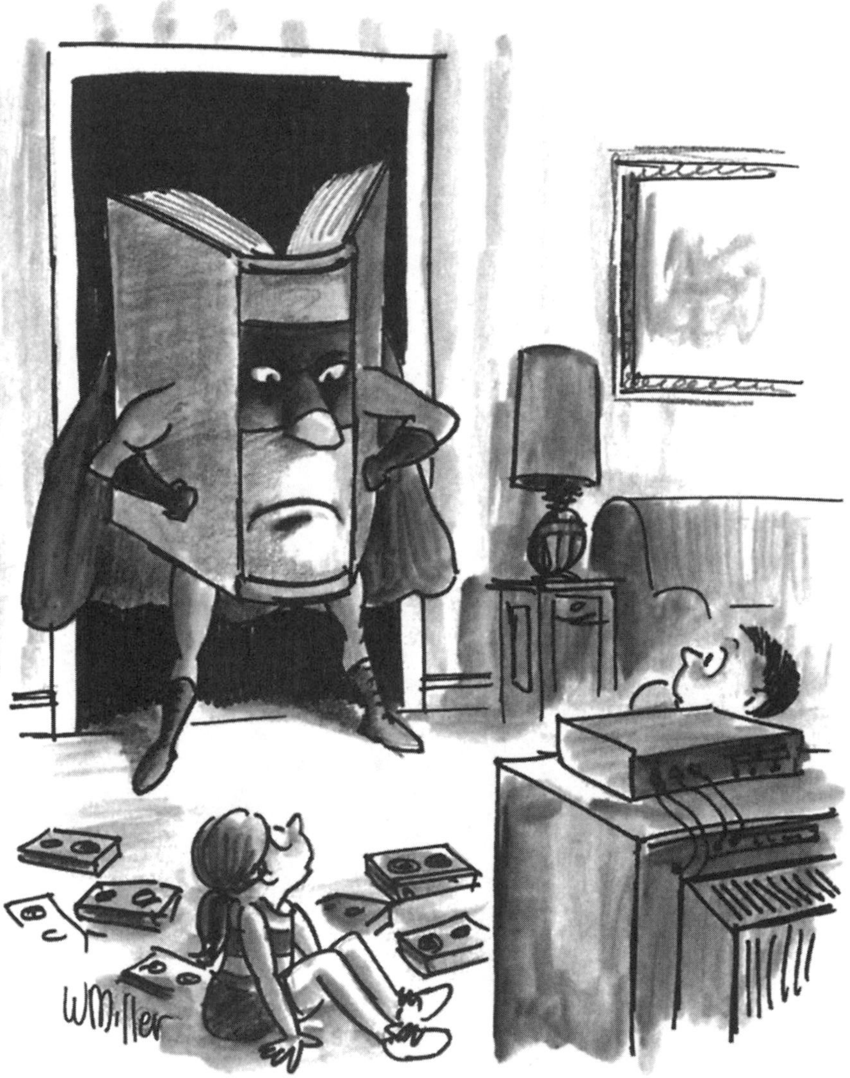
W.Miller

"They can't see you right now—would you like a bottle while you're waiting?"

"Shouldn't Willis be in the bed and his imaginary monster under it?"

"*Do you have any cards for two mommies?*"

"How many thousand do you figure <u>you've</u> eaten?"

"We'd love to come, but we can't seem to find a sitter."

"During the next stage of my development, Dad, I'll be drawing
closer to my mother—I'll get back to you in my teens."

JIMMY, SIXTH-GENERATION PAIN IN THE ASS

"He's swearing in full sentences now."

P.BYRNES.

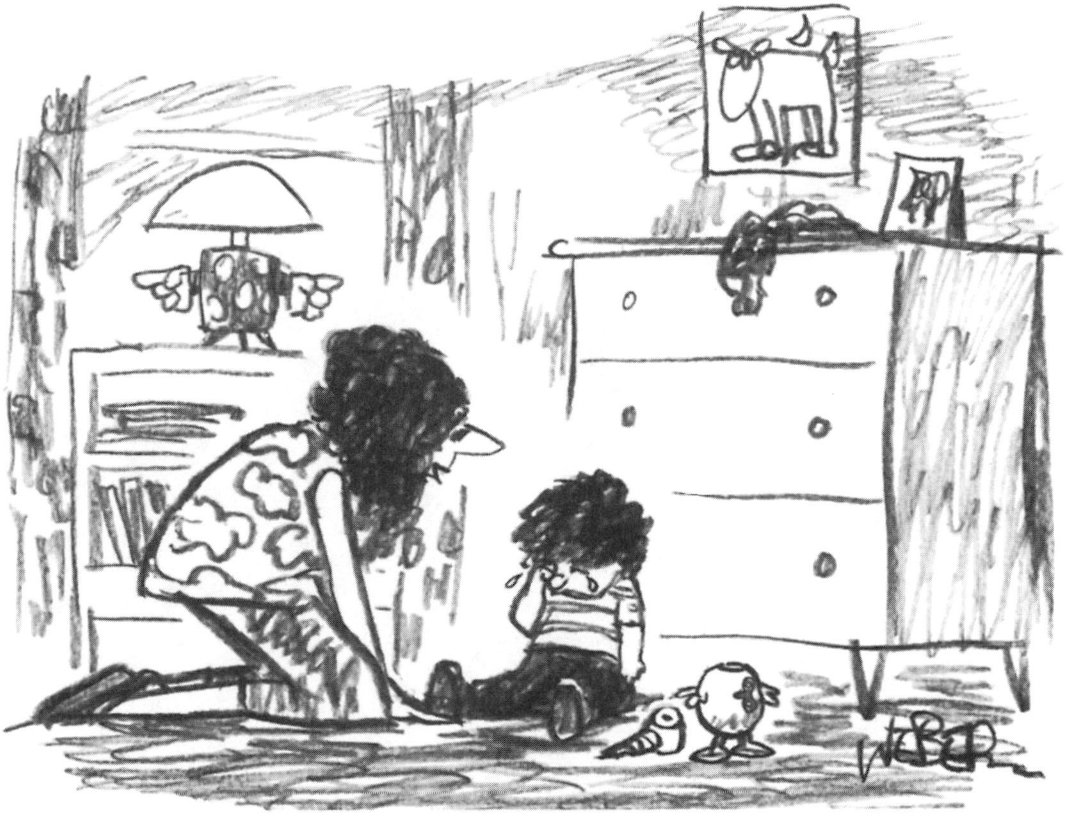
WEBER

"Try verbalizing it."

"If nothing else, school has prepared me for a lifetime of backpacking."

"Five per cent of my income is from lemonade, and the rest is from charity."

"Some women to see you, Anne."

"*Don't cry, Mom. Lots of parents have children who didn't get into their first-choice college,
and they went on to live happy, fulfilled lives.*"

"*Those D's are misleading.*"

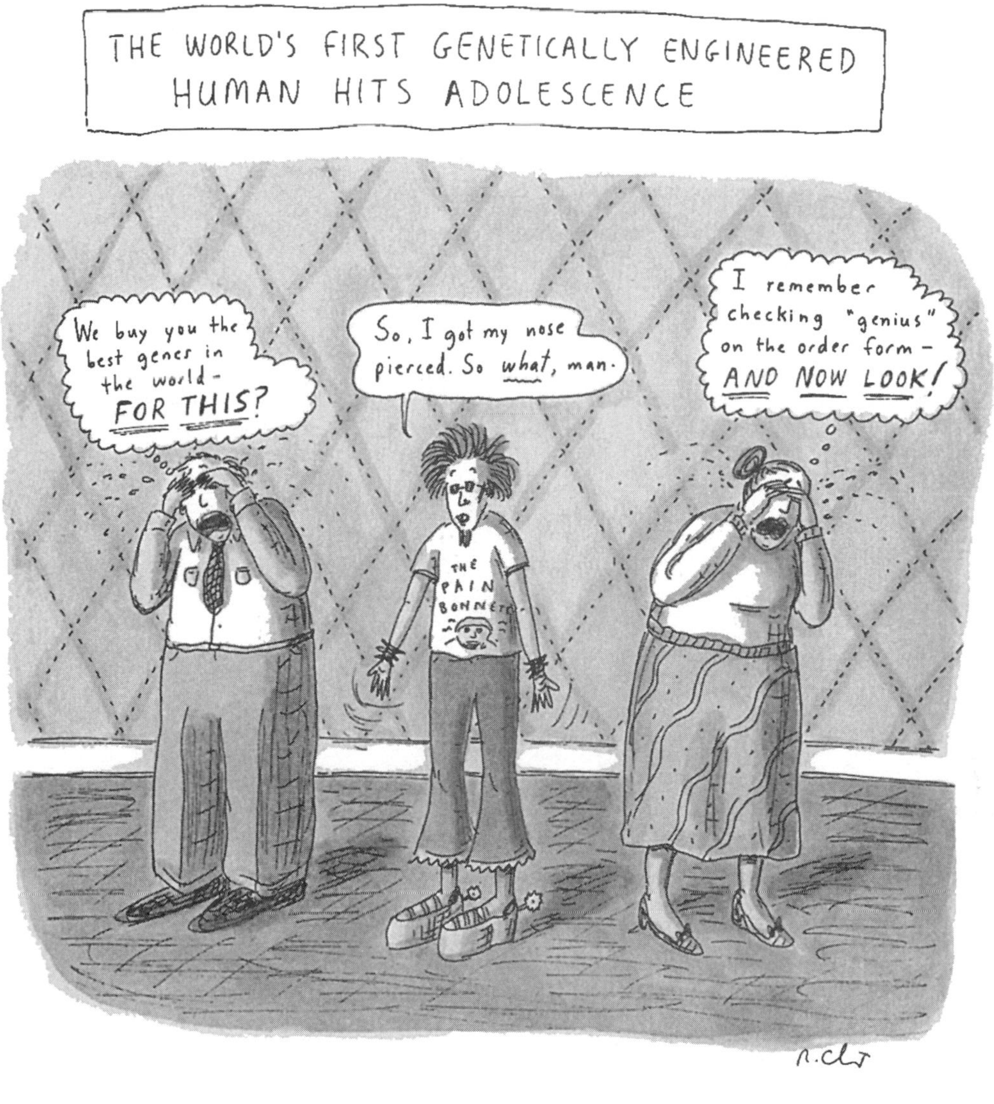
THE WORLD'S FIRST GENETICALLY ENGINEERED HUMAN HITS ADOLESCENCE
We buy you the best genes in the world - FOR THIS?
So, I got my nose pierced. So what, man.
I remember checking "genius" on the order form - AND NOW LOOK!
THE PAIN BONNETS

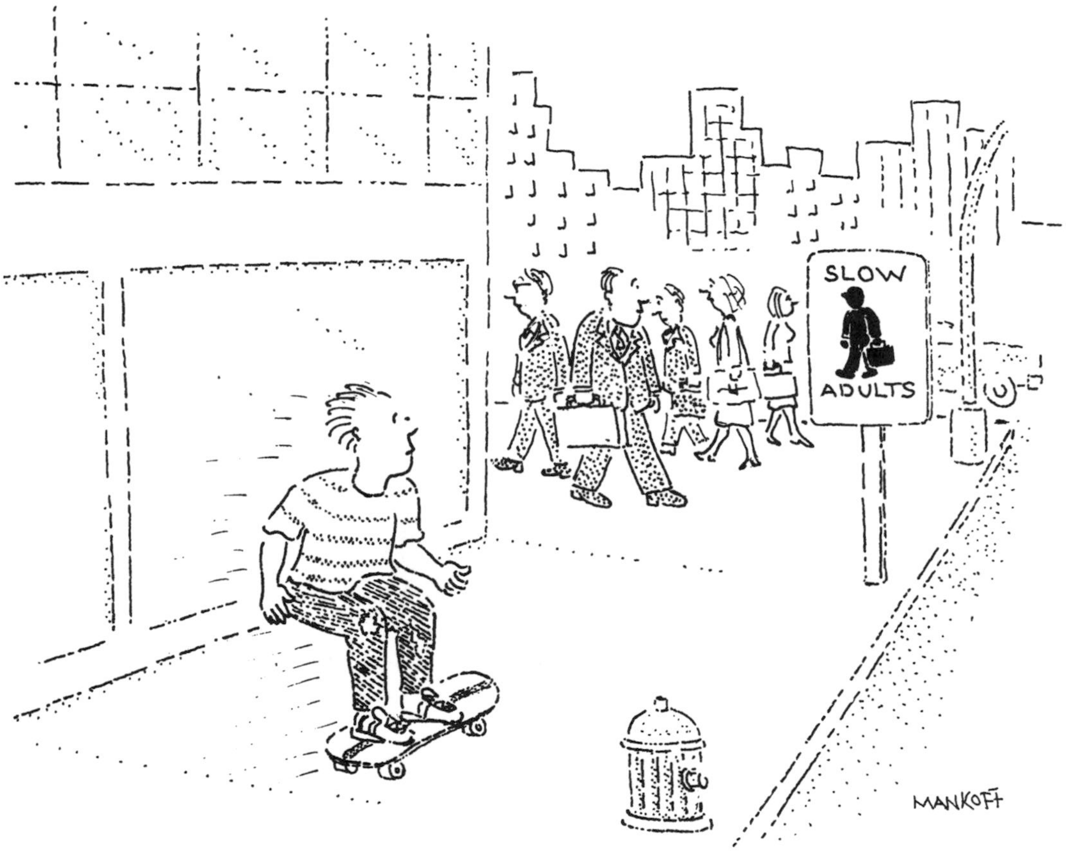
SLOW
ADULTS
MANKOFF

*"Ezra, I'm not inviting you to my birthday party, because our relationship
is no longer satisfying to my needs."*

"How come Jasper's mutual fund is up twelve per cent and mine's only up eight?"

"I see. And precisely what methods did you use to
determine that my client was a 'bad boy'?"

"Jeffrey was a surprise."

"He has some food issues."

"Why does <u>he</u> always get to be the boy?"

"*Would you explain to your son that there's no free agency in T-ball?*"

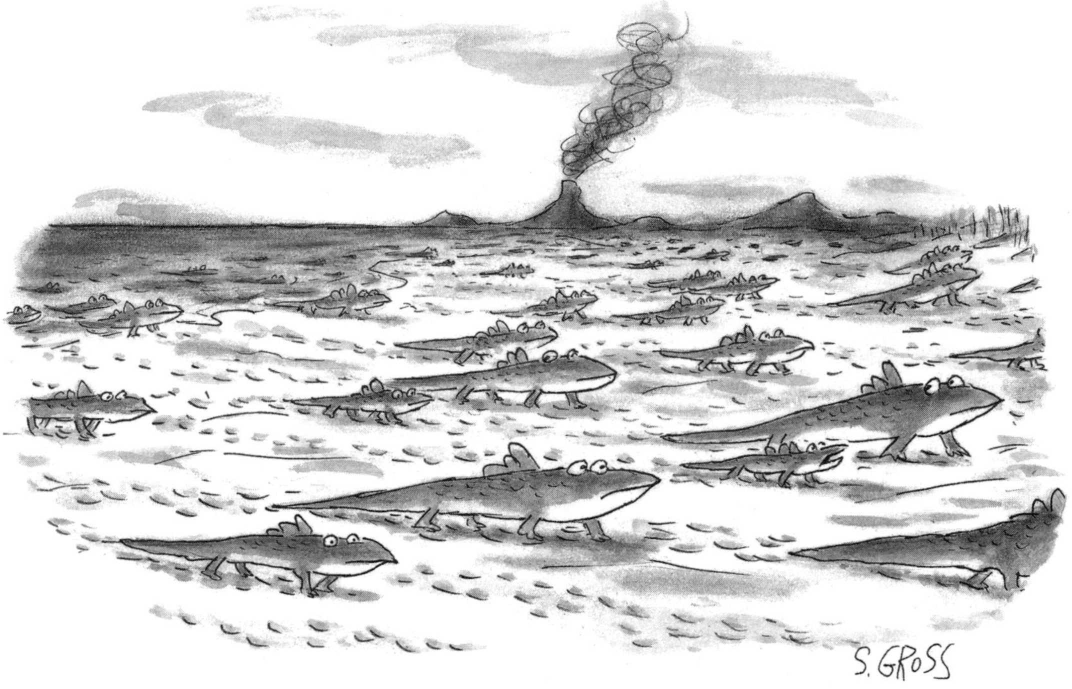
S. GROSS

"Are we there yet?"

CHILDREN'S DREAM BEDTIME ROUTINE

7:30 - 8	Brush teeth; wash hands and face.
8 - 8:30	Get school stuff ready for next day.
8:30 - 9	Put pajamas on.
9 - 11	Watch sitcoms.
11 - 11:30	Watch pro wrestling.
11:30 - 12	Say good night to pets.
12 - 12:30	Midnight snack.
12:30 - 1	Video games.
1 - 1:30	Get into bed.
1:30 - 2:30	Reading hour.
2:30 - 3	Water break.
3 - 4	Read-aloud story time.
4 - 4:30	Last-minute fear assuaging.
4:30	Lights out.

"Son, you're all grown up now. You owe me two hundred and fourteen thousand dollars."

"Yes, the underpants sighting is very interesting, but I'm really more intrigued by your observations of London and France."

"I'm still pre-literate."

"It's the whole kindergarten thing, Mom. I'm alone
in there, swimming with the sharks."

"*Honey, come inside. It's going to take a while to accumulate.*"

"Say, Dad, think you could wrap it up? I have a long day tomorrow."

"Am I the smart one and you're the pretty one or is it the other way around?"

INDEX OF ARTISTS